I0113869

INDOMITABLE SPIRIT

INDOMITABLE

SPIRIT

HOW TO REACT AND SURVIVE
IN A SCHOOL SHOOTING

STEVEN REMY, MS, CPP

Word One Publishing
Chattanooga, Tennessee

Indomitable Spirit: How to React and Survive in a School Shooting

© 2014 Steven Remy

No part of this book may be reproduced in any written, electronic, recording, or photocopying form without written permission of the author. The exception would be in the case of brief quotations embodied in the critical articles or reviews and pages where permission is specifically granted by author.

Although every precaution has been taken to verify the accuracy of the information contained herein, the author and publisher assume no responsibility for any errors or omissions. No liability is assumed for damages that may result from the use of information contained within.

Published in association with Word One Publishing, 1100 Market Street, Floor 6, Chattanooga, Tennessee 37402. For more, visit WordOnePublishing.com.

Trade Paperback ISBN-13: 978-1-945988-03-5

To Leslie, for allowing me to pursue my passions, no matter how perilous, even if it means sleepless nights and restless days for you; and also for helping me to see the various kittens and rainbows in life.

To Sydney and Grayson, for letting me experience how awesome raising two "mini-me's" really is. I love to hear your laughter and see your smiles.

CONTENTS

FOREWORD

The safety of our children, the education and preservation of our future, is the paramount concern of every nation and every civilization. And our children have never been threatened like they are now.

According to the U.S. Dept. of Justice's 2011 report on school crime and safety, there were 57 "school-associated violent deaths" in U.S. schools in 1997. In 2006, we had a new all-time record of 63 violent deaths. *Our children are more likely to be killed by violence in school than all possible causes of death put together!* You will never see that statement in that DOJ report, but I challenge anyone to show me a combination of factors that gave us 63 dead kids in our schools in 2006.

The Sandy Hook elementary school massacre in Newtown, Connecticut, with twenty-one first-graders and six faculty murdered, clearly marked a change. The federal government stopped reporting the data as of that year.

As such, not a single child has been killed by school fire in the U.S. in over 50 years!

We deter these killers. We detect them. We defeat them. And still, every few years we see a new all-time record-high number of children who died as a result of violence in our schools.

Fire experts tell me that in order to meet fire code, you can easily double the construction cost of the school building. Think of it: fireproof material versus a cheaper alternative; fireproof or fire-retardant material for all interior furnishings, paint, flooring and wall-boards; fire sprinkler systems under pressure for the lifetime of the building; and fire exits, fire alarms, fire lights, and smoke alarms wired throughout the building. If you have a six-million-dollar construction cost for a school building, up to three million could be spent on meeting fire code!

If we had children dying and injured from fire they way they are dying from violence, we would turn our world inside-out to prevent this from happening.

In addition to an internal threat to our schools—with children committing mass murders and local citizens coming into our schools to commit mass murders—there is also the potential for an external terrorist threat in our schools.

The possibility of the mass murder of schoolchildren by terrorists is very real. It has happened in many nations already, and terrorists have been able to see the impact school violence has already had in America. One of the worst terrorist acts in modern history was the school massacre in 2004 in Beslan, Russia, where over 300 people were murdered, the vast majority of them children. One of the most tragic and devastating terrorist attacks in Israel was the Ma'alot school massacre. Turkey had over 300 schools attacked in their battle against terrorists. In December 2014, a school in Pakistan was attacked. More than 100 children were massacred, and the following day, every school in Pakistan was closed. These are just some of the tragic, horrific, terrorist attacks upon schools that have occurred around the globe.

Every school day across America, one fifth of the U.S. population is in our schools. No other single institution holds such a large proportion of our population. And it is the most vital, precious, and vulnerable portion of our population: our children, our future.

Nothing is more important than our children and our grandchildren. They are our greatest treasure and our hope for the future. Children are so very weak and vulnerable, yet so filled with vast potential and endless hope for the future. Every child is infinitely precious to someone; therefore each child must be infinitely precious to us all. Thus, the security and safety of our children is the most important function that any society can perform.

Today these precious little ones are threatened, from within and from without, to a greater degree than ever before in living memory. Those who would do us harm—from both inside and outside our borders—know that the path toward the greatest notoriety, and the way to bring the severest suffering to us and to our collective body, is to attack our children. But . . . the sky is not falling. It is completely within our ability to meet this challenge.

You hold in your hands a superb resource, by an eminently qualified author, providing the information you need to help keep our precious children safe. In clear language, quickly and effectively, a true expert and highly respected trainer in the field of school safety has given us the tools to prevent and survive one of these tragic incidents.

This is one of the best books I have read on surviving a rapid mass murder. This book also applies to workplace massacres and acts of mass murder in many other environments.

Let me conclude by explaining why I am so passionate about the field of school safety.

This whole subject first hit my life in 1998, when two boys, ages 11 and 13, gunned down 13 children and two teachers at Westside Middle School in my hometown of Jonesboro, Arkansas. At that point in time it was the all-time record for juvenile mass murder in human history.

I was at the school on the night of the massacre, helping to train the mental health professionals who would work with the teachers and students in the coming days. As a former West Point psychology professor and one of the U.S. Army's experts on PTSD, I was applying the lessons of mass critical incident debriefings learned on the battlefield to my hometown.

A counselor who had been working at the hospital came to the school that night, and she told us a story that brought us all to tears. Clergy and counselors were working in small groups in the hospital waiting room, comforting the groups of relatives and friends of more than a dozen shooting victims. They noticed one woman who had been sitting silently, alone, in the midst of the crowd. A counselor went up to the woman, took her hand, and said, "Can I help you?"

Sitting there in absolute psychological and physiological shock, she said, "I'm the mother of one of the girls who was killed today. They called me and said my little girl is dead. I just came to find out how I can get my little girl back. How do I get her body back?"

She had no friends, no husband, no family with her, and she sat in the hospital, stunned by her loss. But the body had been taken to Little Rock, a hundred miles away, for an autopsy, and she was told that the authorities would contact her when they were finished with the body. Then she could tell them what funeral home to send the body to. After being told this, in a daze, her very next comment was, "Funeral home? Funeral home? We can't afford a funeral. We can't even afford a funeral."

That little girl was truly all the woman had in the world. There were no friends, no family, no husband—just a mama and her little girl. That morning she hugged her little girl, alive and warm and vital, the most precious thing on the face of the earth . . . for the last time. And that night, all she wanted in the world was to wrap her baby's cold body in a blanket and take her home.

Every day, millions of parents hug millions of kids, their most precious possessions, the most precious things on the face of the earth, and they send those kids to school, trusting us to keep them alive. This is the most important thing any society can do: protect our young.

So don't just read this book: study it. Study it and apply it. It could be your child's life that you save.

LT. COL. DAVE GROSSMAN, U.S. Army (Ret.)
Author of *On Killing, On Combat,* and
Stop Teaching Our Kids to Kill
www.killology.com

PREFACE

This book grew out of a series of lectures and training seminars I conducted for hundreds of school educators who were concerned about what to do in the event of a shooting or mass murder attack on their campus. Shortly after a cold-hearted attacker murdered twenty innocent children and six adults at the Sandy Hook Elementary School in Newtown, Connecticut, I quickly came to the realization that many educators either don't think about what to do in situations like this, or choose to think it can't happen to them.

Quality training for these situations seems to be minimal or expensive, which reduces the likelihood that students, teachers, and administrators will react properly if faced with an event like this. Based on my background as a law enforcement officer with formal education in business and organizational security management, I knew I could use my experience to train teachers and students to improve their odds of survival in the event they are ever faced with an armed school attacker.

I have used all of my life experience, training, and education as a well of information to draw from while writing this book. This consists of my time spent as a federal law enforcement officer over the last ten years, along with the formal education I received while obtaining a graduate degree in Business and Organizational Security Management. As a credentialed Certified Protection Professional (CPP) through the American Society of Industrial Security, I study the art and science of security and how to successfully protect children in schools.

This book is a guide for teachers, students, and parents on what to do in the event that their school is attacked by someone whose intent is to inflict harm to as many people as possible.

Simply reading this book, however, does not completely prepare you to respond appropriately to a school attack situation. In addition to this text, you must prepare and mentally rehearse to sharpen your reactions to different situations.

As you will see, your body and mind will not magically rise to the occasion and react as they should when faced with the extreme stress and trauma of someone trying to kill you and your students. Your body and mind will revert to the very basics of what you have trained it to do in an unfortunate situation like this.

Reading this book is your first step in preparing yourself to react quickly and correctly if faced with an armed attacker in your school. With some preparation, you can greatly increase your and your students' chances of survival.

INTRODUCTION

*"One person can make a difference,
and everyone should try."*

—*John F. Kennedy*

School shootings have alarmingly become a part of everyday life in the United States and throughout the world. While some shooters display warning signs prior to their heinous acts, others act in a seemingly random fashion. This makes it increasingly difficult to predict when and where school shootings will happen, which makes it vitally important for school administrators, staff, parents, and students to be prepared to react to these type of events, should they ever happen in their presence.

This book is designed to educate readers

about how to prepare for being caught in a situation where one or more people try to perpetrate the unthinkable crime of attacking vulnerable children in a place where they should be safe—school. I will define what exactly an active shooter is, provide a brief background of previous active shooters and events, describe how the human body responds to extreme stress, discuss the power of mind over body, and provide a framework of what to do and expect during and after, if ever faced with an active shooter situation.

In order to respond in an appropriate manner, you must be exposed to enough information about an active shooter's mindset and tactics to make educated decisions while under stress. One of the keys to minimizing the number of victims in school shootings is preparation by students, teachers, and parents alike.

While it would be ideal for an entire school staff to train and work together in a coordinated fashion, the reality is that only a few staff in each school may take the time to educate themselves about school attackers and how they should counter any threats they may face. However, in this type of situation, one properly educated person can make an enormous difference in the lives of others.

CHAPTER ONE: ACTIVE SHOOTER DEFINITION AND HISTORY

Many people have heard the term "active shooter" used throughout the media and may not have a complete understanding of exactly what the term means. An active shooter is a person actively engaged in killing or attempting to kill people inside a structure or outside in a populated area, with the intent of mass murder, as opposed to other criminal conduct, such as robbery or assault. The event itself is considered to be a low probability yet high-consequence occurrence.

Active shooters have been targeting innocent

people for many years. Schools are targeted specifically because they are especially vulnerable and have a high shock value. Many perpetrators are mentally ill and vary in their reasons for attacking others. Some are even copycat offenders who pre-plan shootings to make what they believe are grand statements or to top the last shooter they saw in the media. Regardless of their reasons, school attackers are part of a profile of offenders who seek to kill large amounts of helpless victims who are unable to fight back; in addition to schools, these places include elderly living facilities, hospitals, and daycare centers.

Thorough research shows that an accurate profile of an active shooter, based on common characteristics, does not exist. Perpetrators vary from each other in various ways, with the exception that 94 percent were male, according to research conducted by ALERRT.[1] ALERRT's research also showed that from 2000–2012, the youngest shooter was thirteen years old, while the oldest shooter was eighty-eight years old. Many perpetrators of these crimes would be considered to be (or perceive themselves as being) powerless in their lives and shooting innocent people in a school is a last act of power in which they are able to determine who lives and who dies. A great number of these shooters will commit suicide when confronted or pressured by resistance from victims or law enforcement.

An increasingly common trend shows that some school attackers are kids lashing back with acts of violence against others who bully them. Motives for school shootings range from attention, suicide, desire for revenge, and an overwhelming feeling of being bullied, persecuted, or threatened by others. Often times the shooter's motive is likely a combination of the above. According to the Safe School Initiative Report[2], 93 percent of attackers planned their attack in advance and had also engaged in some sort of behavior prior to the attack that caused others to be concerned. The most disturbing data was the report's revelation that in 80 percent of school shootings, at least one person had information that the attacker was thinking about or planning the attack. In nearly all of these cases, the person who knew was a peer, friend, schoolmate, or sibling.

While the school shootings that have taken place in the United States over the last few decades are atrocious, they pale in comparison to various school shootings across the globe. The worst recorded school shooting in the United

States took place in Michigan in 1927 at the Bath Consolidated School. In this event, the perpetrator killed 38 children, 4 teachers, and 2 others (including his wife) through the use of firearms and explosives. In comparison, armed terrorists seized a school for three days in Beslan, North Ossetia, Russia. A total of 186 children and 199 adults were murdered, and another 783 injured. Many of these victims, children and adults alike, were beaten, tortured, raped, starved, and burned to death.

Nigeria has also become a hotbed of mass murders in schools in recent history. Terrorist groups have been conducting well-coordinated attacks on schools that often result in gruesome deaths of innocent children that make even the worst school shooting in the United States look like child's play. These groups have been known to herd victims into an enclosed area, douse them with gasoline, and light them on fire to achieve high body counts. These are the threats our children face across the world, and as it is well known that the United States is not immune to bold terrorist attacks conducted by religious extremists.

Many people often think of the school shooting that took place in Columbine, Colorado, in 1999, as the first of the modern era that brought then-existing law enforcement response tactics into question. In their initial response to Columbine High School, some of the first officers on scene exchanged gunfire with one of the shooters, who then retreated back into the school. Responding officers then secured the perimeter of the school and awaited the arrival of a Special Weapons and Tactics (SWAT) team, as they were trained to do. From there, it took the SWAT team nearly 45 minutes to arrive, assemble, and enter the school. During this time, the shooters were able to murder 12 students, 1 teacher, and injure an additional 24. Given the large span of time the murderers had, it's astounding that more students and teachers weren't killed. The reality of the situation is not a reflection of the character of the responding officers; it is simply a representation of the training they were operating under at the time of the event.

One of the most recent school active shooter events took place at Sandy Hook Elementary school in Newtown, Connecticut. In this situation, the perpetrator murdered a total of 20 defenseless children and 6 adults before law enforcement could enter the school. This is the unfortunate new reality that school teachers and students face. But we don't have to face this reality unprepared.

CHAPTER TWO:
EARLY DETECTION OF POTENTIAL SCHOOL ATTACKERS

Believe it or not, many school attackers exhibit obvious signs of their intentions well before they carry out their atrocious acts. These assailants will often tell a close friend or peer, and have even been known to publicly post their plans on social media websites. These actions often result from a desire of the perpetrator to seek attention and make a name for themselves. As we learned earlier from the Safe School Initiative Report, in around 80 percent of school shootings at least one person had information that the attacker was thinking about or planning the school attack.

In October 2012, a high school student in the Dallas metropolitan area detailed a theoretical mass shooting attack at the high school he attended on his social media account. Excerpts from the posting included: "go find the police, say I need both their help in the band room, act like it's a fight, walk in, shoot them both," and, "mapped out the entire school and how to do it." The posting laid out a comprehensive plan that involved killing school resource officers, shooting students, and setting off bombs as diversionary devices. The good news in this story is that a concerned student reported the posting to authorities that later arrested the student responsible for the threat. Without the responsible actions of the student who reported the information, another school shooting would likely have happened within a few weeks of the posting. Thankfully, pre-attack detection like this occurs more often than people realize and more often than the media reports.

In order to effectively detect and deter potential school attacks, schools and school districts should have reporting mechanisms in place that children and adults are comfortable with using. Unfortunately not all individuals are comfortable reporting information to school administrators or law enforcement. Some fear they might be viewed as paranoid, while others worry about reporting inaccurate information and wasting law enforcement's time and resources. Additionally, some people fear retaliation; others don't take threats or suspicious activity seriously, or might even be uncertain of whom to tell.

Anonymous tip lines are an excellent way for students, teachers, parents, and concerned citizens to report threats and other suspicious activities. Tip lines can either be manned by live call takers or just voicemail systems that notify personnel of new messages. Particularly successful tip lines can even provide both options so callers can choose whichever method makes them the most comfortable. With the prevalence of digital devices like smart phones, tablets, and computers, tip lines should also incorporate the ability to email or text message tips. By casting the widest net and allowing multiple streams of information in, tip lines have proven to be an inexpensive and effective tool time and time again.

Individual teachers should discuss tip lines with their supervisors and school board members. Teachers who are fortunate enough to have a School Resource Officer assigned to their campus have the opportunity to speak directly to their officer about the availability of tip lines. It can be especially helpful if teachers inform their students that teachers can be trusted to listen to students' concerns without fear of judgment or retaliation. If students understand they can share suspicions, fears, and concerns about other students with responsible adults, the likelihood of pre-attack intervention increases.

While anyone who hears threats or sees suspicious activities can use tip lines as a method of reporting, teachers and other faculty are frequently privy to some of the deepest and darkest secrets that students share while fulfilling school assignments: artwork and writing. As previously mentioned, children who make the decision to commit violent acts against their peers and teachers often need an outlet for their thoughts. In some cases, this outlet is telling friends in person or posting threats online. In other cases, however, this need manifests itself through school writing and art assignments. These revelations are referred to as "leakage" in the Federal Bureau of Investigation's[3] school shooter threat assessment resource. The FBI also articulates that leakage is considered to be one of the most important clues that may precede an adolescent's violent act.

Specific to the mass murder of students at Virginia Tech University in 2007, the armed attacker who was a current student at Virginia Tech at the time of the shootings, had been regularly submitting inappropriate and violent academic writings since he was in middle school. According to the report of the Virginia Tech Review Panel[4], the assailant had submitted an academic writing product for one of his classes that detailed "a young man who hates the students at his school and plans to kill them and himself." Vecchi[5] reported in an academic article that the attacker's creative writing class had dwindled from 70 to 7 students because of the behavior he displayed in class and the content of his writings. In the case of Virginia Tech, warning signs were everywhere, with some of them being reported to a fractured web of law enforcement and academic faculty. Though he had been monitored by school faculty and for a while, mental health professionals, the splintered nature of the reporting resulted in no significant action being taken by law enforcement or the university to appropriately address the murderer's telling behavior prior to his rampage.

Excessive and abnormal violence displayed in a student's writings and artwork should be taken just as serious as direct verbal threats and reported immediately to administrators and parents, and possibly even law enforcement. It is important for teachers to understand how to identify inappropriate concepts and topics in youth writing and artwork, such as violence, suicide, homicide, substance abuse, and other criminal behavior. Most youth don't "snap" or suddenly become violent based on a single event. A series of events often leads to breaking points with warning signs along the way. Teachers should monitor the content of student's writings, drawings, and conversations for any signs of violence. Teachers should also be careful to view these things within the context of which they are contained. For example, a student who writes a story about killing a deer with a rifle while on a hunting trip with his father should be seen differently from a student who draws a picture of himself killing students at a football game with a rifle. The latter should certainly draw increased scrutiny from school officials, law enforcement, and parents.

Although not often reported in any significant depth by the media, some school attacks have been averted as a result of information shared through tip lines and information sharing. Once such successful example of this happened in May 1999 in Port Huron, Michigan. A group of four middle school students ranging in age from twelve to fourteen years old were caught planning an extravagant attack at their school, in which they allegedly planned to detonate a bomb, shoot and kill as many students as possible, and even rape female students. This attack was stopped before any action was taken, when a fourteen-year-old peer overheard the group discussing their plan and how it would outdo the attack that took place at Columbine High School earlier that year. Fortunately this fellow student had the courage to inform authorities about what she overheard, and the four students were arrested one day before they were scheduled to conduct their attack. One young student's courage to do the right thing changed the course of history for many families that day.

CHAPTER THREE: THE HUMAN BODY'S RESPONSE TO STRESS

It is important to understand the human body's response to extreme stress so that you will have a framework of what physiological changes you will be dealing with in the event you are faced with an attack on your school. When faced with extreme stress, fear, or trauma, people typically react in one of three ways: fight, flight, or freeze.

During and after an extremely stressful event, such as being faced with an armed attacker, your body may experience a wide array of effects that commonly include:

- tunnel vision
- auditory exclusion (unable to hear things)
- slow motion
- amnesia (periods with no memory)
- increased heart rate
- loss of fine motor skills
- extreme thirst

These and others are a result of your body's physiological preparation and exertion to handling the stress you are faced with. Your body and your actions will revert to what you have trained for and rehearsed, both mentally and physically. I can say through my own first-hand experience, I felt the effects of all of the above stress responses when I was personally involved in an on-duty shooting and use of deadly force incident while attempting to arrest a violent fugitive. I was well prepared to handle my body's responses to the stress, and I was still surprised at how my body responded at the time.

Professional athletes don't become experts in their chosen sport based on natural ability alone; they train and practice consistently until they develop high-level skill sets that make them competitive. Part of this training involves under-standing how their bodies and minds behave under the stress of competition. With enough self-reflection, education, and training, anyone can alter how their bodies react in stressful situations. This is the primary reason why it is so important to prepare yourself for a scenario in which you and your students are faced with an armed attacker.

You will likely experience many of these aforementioned conditions and effects during the stressful event itself. Additional conditions and symptoms may present themselves imme-diately after the event, while more may appear during the days and weeks following the event. Being aware of these will help you understand what your body is doing through the course of the incident, as well as after. Understanding that these physiological reactions are completely normal will also help with your emotional healing process.

Years of scientific studies focusing on police officers involved in deadly-force shoot-ings allows us to see how the human body responds to life-threatening situations. One of these researchers, Seymour Epstein[6], revealed that humans generally have two different modes of processing information: a rational-thinking mode and an experiential-thinking mode.

The rational-thinking mode is how humans process a majority of the information they come into contact with during everyday life. This mode of thought allows for deliberative, conscious, and analytical cognitive processing that typically characterizes what most people understand as rational thinking.

As an example, your brain processes an uneventful day at work in rational-thinking mode. You handle day-to-day decisions by thinking through your problems, carefully and thoughtfully weighing the benefits and consequences of your actions, and researching options on how to best react to situations you are faced with in uneventful daily life. Essentially, the bulk of your daily life is spent in a rational-thinking mode.

The more relevant type of thinking during a high-stress situation, like being involved in a violent attack, is the experiential-thinking mode. Epstein characterized experiential-thinking as the body's way of "automatically, rapidly, effortlessly, and efficiently processing information." This way of thinking essentially allows for the human body to react rapidly to stressful and

life-threatening situations. This mode of information processing is more efficient and takes less
effort, which is why the human body reverts to
this type of processing during traumatic events.

Experiential thinking is more simply viewed
as reactionary in nature. For example, imagine
yourself walking from the front door of your
house to your mailbox to mail a letter. You see a
group of children playing baseball in the street
and suddenly you see a baseball accidentally hit
in your direction. As the baseball approaches
the general area of your head, your body automatically responds by sending your hands and
arms to shield your head from the baseball,
while the rest of your body instinctively ducks to
decrease your overall size. This is a non-complex
example of experiential thinking. Through past
experiences you understand that hard objects
flying at your head are not good for your health.
You also know that your arms and hands serve
as excellent shields from such objects. Due to
the speed of events, it is not possible for you to
rationally process how to appropriately respond.
You don't have time to weigh if the baseball traveling in the direction of your head is an actual
baseball or a harmless Wiffle ball. You also don't
have time to analyze if the baseball is actually

going to hit your head or just fly harmlessly over it. This experiential-thinking mode allows you to react quickly and efficiently to the fast-paced or highly stressful stimulus you are faced with.

One of the main characteristics of experiential-thinking is that it is based on past experiences, versus a real-time intake of current events. What this essentially means is that your reactions to current stimuli during a high-stress event will often be dictated on past experiences. Although experiential-thinking is what happens when your body "naturally" reacts to something, just like a professional athlete who trains his body and mind, you can change your natural reaction to stress and trauma. If you want to react in the most effective manner, you must prepare and train yourself to do so.

Since the vast majority of people never experience any sort of life-threatening event throughout their lifetime, their bodies don't have any data to draw on when they revert to experiential thinking. Others have reverted to this kind of thinking when they experience something instantaneous that they perceive to be a life-or-death situation. A common example of this would be a narrowly avoided collision while driving. These types of occurrences are fairly common and range from drivers instinctively swerving to avoid large animals in the road, or drivers slamming on their brakes to avoid being hit by a vehicle that has run a red light.

The only way to give your brain data to work with while it is in experiential-thinking mode is to mentally prepare, rehearse scenarios in your head, and physically participate in training where you are forced to determine your best course of action when reacting to an armed attack. When you face these types of split-second decisions, you can learn from your own natural reaction. If your reaction worked to avoid harm, you are more likely to have the same reaction in the future to a similar situation. If your reaction did not serve its intended purpose of avoiding harm, you'll have the ability to evaluate the incident in hindsight and determine what your best course of action should have been. Based on this evaluation, you can then incorporate this experience and draw from it in future occurrences. The more you have physically and mentally prepared yourself for a situation, the more likely you are to respond in the proper way.

Anyone who has learned a new skill or practiced a sport has probably heard the phrase, "practice makes perfect." An excellent way to strengthen your retention of new information or behavior is to use as many of your senses as possible during your practice and rehearsal. For example, physically locating all the exits in your school will be more effective than just looking at them on a school map. Physically walking your students through lockdown and escape drills is more effective than simply telling them what do or having them read it in a handout.

Other research conducted by Alexis Artwohl, Ph.D.[7] has shown that 74 percent of officers studied stated that they responded to deadly-force shootings in "automatic pilot," with little or no conscious thought. This "automatic pilot" the officers responded with is highly reflective of experiential-thinking, which processes information so efficiently that the officers felt as if their reaction was automatic and took no conscious thought or effort.

While on the surface it may seem that you are fighting for your life and the lives of your students against all odds, a little forethought, training, and practice can truly make a life-saving difference. Preparing yourself not only helps you remember what you need to do if you are attacked, it will also increase your ability to function and think while your body is under extreme stress. Minimizing the negative effects and harnessing the positive aspects of your body's adrenaline rush can be accomplished and used to your advantage.

CHAPTER FOUR:
MENTAL AND PHYSICAL PREPARATION

In times of extreme stress, your brain typically will not function in the most efficient manner, thus making it difficult to think. In order to respond appropriately in a high-stress situation, you must train, prepare, rehearse, and drill. One of the options we will discuss later is to escape from the building or area where an attacker is trying to kill people. In order to do this in an efficient manner, you must know all the details of the building(s) within which you work. You need to know all entrances and exits, classrooms, offices, storage closets, restrooms, gathering areas, as well as which doors do and do not lock, and the times doors are typically locked during school hours. In addition to knowing the layout of your school building, you must also be able to quickly recall all of this information at a time when your mind will be racing with thoughts of what to do. Touring your school as a group of teachers and administrators with your janitorial staff will allow everyone to educate themselves about the layout of the school. Looking at a map of the building is helpful, but occasionally physically touring and seeing every corner of the facility will be extremely beneficial for information retention. Depending on the size of your school and campus, it's a good idea to do this at least three to four times per year. This is also a great time to discuss possible escape routes with your fellow teachers.

While discussing the escape routes, it is a good time to discuss lockdown and emergency drills, and also role-play specific scenarios among teachers and other faculty. If your school is assigned a School Resource Officer (SRO) or other law enforcement officer, having them present will be beneficial as well. A properly trained and proactive SRO can be extremely helpful with drill planning and execution. With the entire staff together, it is also important to decide on an internal communication plan in the event of an armed attacker. Does your school have a PA system? When was the last time it was used or tested? Do teachers carry around handheld radios to communicate with each other? However your school is designed, you must decide on the best method of internal communication as a faculty team. If gunshots are heard outside, someone needs to communicate to all teachers within the school about the situation. We will talk more about this in the next section that focuses on your response options.

Mentally running through scenarios will help get you in the proper mindset of how to appropriately respond to a school shooter situation. You should also consider your physical and psychological condition and contemplate what you are physically and mentally willing and capable of doing, if you are ever faced with one of these situations.

If you are like most people, you probably have a hard time coming up with realistic scenarios to place yourself in to visualize or rehearse your actions. An excellent source of ideas can be found on a daily basis by watching your local evening news. When you hear about crimes that occur in your area, mentally place yourself in the victim's shoes and work through exactly how you would respond. These types of mental activities help provide your brain with data to draw from when it reverts to experiential-thinking mode in high-stress situations.

You can also run through scenarios during an in-service day at school with your peers or at home with your family. Start with a simple scenario in which a teacher pretending to be an attacker enters the front entrance of your school. No elaborate acting or props are required; your imagination should be enough to carry you through. Communication should begin when the first teacher or staff member sees the attacker, simulates calling 9-1-1, and informs the entire school of the situation. Teachers in their classrooms should immediately begin executing their plans to evacuate their students and communicate amongst each other.

To advance past the most basic of scenarios highlighted above, work with your local police department or SRO to add layers of complexity to your training. This can involve having officers respond to and enter your school during a drill to see how teachers and law enforcement work together in situations.

Not all schools are fortunate enough to have a dedicated SRO from a local police department assigned full-time to the school. Many schools only have part-time SROs, while others don't have anyone assigned at all. Regardless of your school's SRO status, school administrators can take steps to create a positive relationship between the school and the local police department. Cooperation between schools and their respective police departments can create a win-win situation for each other. Police departments are constantly looking for new and unique places within their jurisdictions to train officers on various tactics. Schools benefit when local officers know the architecture and layout of the entire building. When schools work with police departments to allow officers to train as groups during weekend or after-school hours, everybody wins.

An often-overlooked yet basic preparation step is how to dial 9-1-1 from your school's landline telephone. Does your phone system require you to dial "9" to reach an outside line? If so, is it also required when you dial 9-1-1 or only when you dial a 7- or 10-digit phone number? The time to figure this all out is before your body is under severe stress—not in the midst of chaos.

A teacher-friend of mine recently relayed a story in which she had difficulty dialing 9-1-1 from her school's landline phone. A fellow teacher had suddenly become severely ill at school and an ambulance was needed. When she attempted to dial 9-1-1, she was met with a fast busy signal. Remembering that her school's phone system required her to dial "9" to reach an outside line, she dialed 9, then 9-1-1, but was again met with a fast busy signal. Understanding time was of the essence, she dialed 9-1-1 from her cell phone, was passed around to at least two dispatch centers, and finally connected to her local emergency dispatch center. It was later determined for unknown technical reasons, the school's phone system was unable to dial 9-1-1. Though now rectified, this situation could have gone from bad to worse very quickly, especially if her school had been under attack by an armed individual.

Based on this teacher's experience, I always suggest that schools conduct a test of their phone systems by calling 9-1-1 at least once per year. This is something that can easily be coordinated by calling your local police department's non-emergency phone number during normal business hours, and asking them what steps you need to take to conduct a test of your 9-1-1 phone system.

Most likely they will notify their 9-1-1 call center that a test call is scheduled and you can dial 9-1-1 to test connectivity. Once you test the system and confirm it works as designed, take the time and remind all teachers and faculty how to dial 9-1-1 from the school's landline. Don't assume that everyone knows how to successfully complete an emergency phone call, especially if your system requires users to dial anything to reach an outside line. Inserting a short training block into your required annual in-service training is a quick and easy way to accomplish this.

By preparing yourself both mentally and physically, you increase your chances of quickly responding to a stressful situation in a manner that gives you the best outcome. Remember to do the following to help with preparation:

- Occasionally walk through your school and explore areas you don't visit often. Familiarize yourself with these areas and every entrance and exit of the building. Look for potential hiding spots and escape routes throughout.

- Review your school's lockdown policies and procedures and participate in lockdown drills conducted by your school.
- Role-play different scenarios with your peers within your school building. Extend an invitation to participate to your SRO or local police department.
- Test the internal communication system (PA system, handheld radios, etc.) your school administrators have identified as applicable for lockdown or active attack situations. If one has not been identified, make a positive change and suggest one.
- With the help and coordination of your local police department, test your school's landline telephone system by conducting a test of its 9-1-1 dialing capabilities.

CHAPTER FIVE: PHYSICAL SECURITY

Assailants who are in the planning stages of their attack will look for particularly weak targets among schools. Buildings and facilities that adhere to quality physical security standards and procedures are considered to be "hard" targets; those that follow lax standards or no standards at all are considered to be "soft" targets. Attackers will watch the area and look for any weaknesses in physical security, such as open doors or lax visitor policies. These mass murderers' only fear in life at this point is not successfully carrying out their attack. With this in mind, they will move from school to school looking for the softest target that has the highest likelihood for success. It is extremely important for schools and school districts not only to implement stringent security policies, but also to ensure all policies are being followed appropriately and taking strong corrective action when deficiencies in execution are found.

First and foremost, all interior classroom and office doors should be lockable from within the classroom or office without the use of a key. While in session, these doors should remain closed and locked as well. In addition to lockable classroom doors, all exterior doors should be kept locked and secured during school hours. Exterior doors should never be propped open unless directly monitored by a dedicated staff member who is physically present during events such as recess or other outdoor activities. These two things should be non-negotiable when dealing with requests to modify existing security measures or building security measures into new construction. A single point of entry to the school during school hours is important to implement so that access to your campus is secured and controlled as much as possible.

The only event in which it is acceptable to prop doors open without a dedicated observer is during a fire drill or when the fire alarm to the building is activated. It exists within the realm of possibilities that an attacker could pull a fire alarm to lure students outside of their class-rooms and school building in an effort to open fire on them from an area outside of the school. If this happens and exit doors are closed and locked shut, it impedes the students' ability to retreat into the safety of the school if an attacker is located outside. Even though doors should be propped open during these limited circum-stances, a faculty member should still keep an eye on their closest exit to make sure no one enters through the propped open doors while others are exiting.

Another vulnerability of schools rests within the mode of transportation that the vast major-ity of students take to and from school every day—the school bus. In 1976, three armed men in Chowchilla, California, hijacked a school bus with one driver and twenty-six children. The bus driver and all twenty-six children were held underground for sixteen hours until the driver managed to find an escape route for him and the children. School bus hijackings have happened on numerous occasions in the United States, which shows busses may even be easier targets than physical school buildings.

Most recently, in January 2013 a single armed gunman in Midland City, Alabama, boarded a school bus, killed the driver, and took a child hostage from the bus. The attacker held the child for nearly a week in an underground bunker before law enforcement was able to successfully save the child and kill the assailant. Information about the attack revealed the attacker may have boarded the bus unexpectedly, to the surprise of the driver. Once aboard, the attacker informed the driver he was going to take several children hostage, at which point the driver physically challenged him; unfortunately for the driver, the attacker had a firearm and killed the driver in order to carryout his kidnapping. Because of situations like this, bus drivers should never let unauthorized individuals board their bus, if at all possible. Not every type of attack is completely avoidable, but following certain procedures can greatly reduce the chances of attacks in general.

It is important for schools and school districts to create and implement strict security policies for bus drivers to follow when they have children aboard. This includes policies that prohibit drivers from stopping to help motorists who appear to be broken down on the side of the road, or stopping for anyone waving them down. Thinking in these terms can help to harden school busses as a target for mass murderers. Teachers and faculty should also look for suspicious individuals or instances around their school and in the parking lot while monitoring school bus drop-off and pick-up.

Most school attackers either have direct knowledge of the facility they are going to attack, either through previous visits to the campus for legitimate reasons, or through conducting surveillance on the target location. Surveillance is a huge indicator of a potential attack. Therefore all suspicious incidents around schools should immediately be reported to local police. Something as simple as requiring teachers who are on a break-period to walk around the school building and through the parking lot can make a world of a difference. If they see an occupied vehicle for an extended period of time near their school or in the parking lot, a simple call to local law enforcement can deter potential attackers. This will let the would-be perpetrator know that their chances of successfully attacking that specific school are significantly less than what they were hoping for. Staying alert and aware and communicating with local law enforcement works wonders for the security of your school and your students.

It should also be noted that schools and school districts should strictly prohibit discussing specific security measures over the telephone. Parents of current or future students who have security concerns should be directed to make a personal appointment with an appropriate administrator or school resource officer to discuss their concerns. Standard practice should be informing the caller that you are not permitted to discuss security-related information over the phone and offering to schedule a meeting for the caller with the appropriate security official. Providing sensitive security information over the phone to anonymous individuals can prove fatal if it falls into the wrong hands. Suspicious callers inquiring about security information should also be reported to local law enforcement or your school resource officer. These tests of security are often indicators of potential future attacks; providing detailed information to law enforcement about these types of occurrences can lead to preventing attacks.

CHAPTER SIX:
RESPONSE TO AN
ACTIVE SHOOTER

If ever faced with an active shooter situation, you have three primary options: escape, deny access, or fight. Various governmental agencies and private organizations will sometimes refer to these three options with different terminology but the fundamentals of the actions are generally the same. Each and every active shooter scenario is different and no single response is always the best response, depending on the specific circumstances of the attack. Individuals should handle the situation and respond with the information available to them at the time of the incident.

Active shooter situations are unpredictable and evolve rapidly, often changing circumstances from second to second. For this reason, it is important to understand that what may have been the right decision ten seconds ago may no longer make sense. Considering there is no perfect answer for any situation like this, you must determine the best course of action to protect yourself and the lives of your students and peers. Whatever decision you make, it is imperative that you stay calm and think clearly, because your students will cue off of your reactions. Again, if you want the children you are responsible for to remain calm, you yourself must also remain calm and assure them that they are safe as long as they are with you and they listen to everything you tell them to do.

In a situation like this, it is absolutely necessary to make quality decisions quickly, often times with minimal information. In most cases, there is not a single correct answer and a multitude of options will likely lead to the same outcome. The ability to quickly make decisions with minimal information will be increased if you have mentally rehearsed for high-stress situations and envisioned reasonable steps to take. Without rehearsal, drills, and mental preparation, you greatly reduce your chances of making the right decisions in a short amount of time. The worst possible thing you can do during a mass-murder situation is to make no decision and freeze during the event. Freezing and inaction will likely make matters worse for you, your peers, and the children you are responsible for protecting.

As with many things in life, clear and effective communication to the right people is key to a positive outcome. At the very first signs of trouble (i.e., hearing gunshots, witnessing an armed individual threatening others etc.), it is imperative that you dial 911 to notify law enforcement immediately. The earlier law enforcement is contacted, the quicker they will arrive and eliminate the threat. Depending on your local jurisdiction, you may not be directly connected to your local police department or sheriff's office when you dial 911, either from your cell phone or a landline at your school. Many departments participate in regional 911 dispatching systems, meaning your call will arrive at a centralized dispatch facility, which may or may not be in your area, who will then direct your call to the proper law enforcement agency depending on the information you provide to them. While these regional centers are great for shrinking local budgets, they can wreak havoc on communication delays and law enforcement response times. While a few seconds here and there might not sound like a lot, when you consider that every second that passes during an armed school attack is at least one additional death, seconds really do count.

Law enforcement officers will do their absolute best to make it to your location as quickly as possible to eliminate the threat, but it may take several minutes for them to even be dispatched to your location with accurate information. Once again, what you do while you are waiting for law enforcement to arrive is key to the survival of yourself and the children you are responsible for. You have more control than you may think in an armed attack, but you must be prepared to act appropriately.

When you first hear shots or encounter an armed individual in your school, you must assess the situation and decide your best course of action. Specifically, you should:

- Assess your surroundings and decide to escape, deny access, or fight; quickly begin to take action to accomplish the option you decided on.

- Determine the best way to communicate the situation with law enforcement authorities, either through the use of a nearby landline phone or your cell phone.
- Communicate the situation to your students and any peers who are in your immediate vicinity.
- Continuously reassess the situation based on current information and change your response as necessary.

When you are connected to the proper 9-1-1 dispatch center, you must clearly and concisely describe what is happening, the location of your school, and any identifying information you have about the perpetrator. With your adrenaline pumping and heart rate high, this will not be an easy task. Consciously slowing down your breathing into steady and deep rhythms will help slow your heart rate and make your communication more effective.

It is important to relay what the attacker is wearing and where the attacker currently is located. An ideal communication would look like this: "I am calling from Jones Elementary School in Dallas and there is an older white male shooting at students in the gymnasium. He is wearing a green t-shirt, blue jeans, and a black hat. It looks like he has a handgun and is wearing a black backpack." The dispatcher may further clarify your actual address within a few seconds, but it is important to relay the fact that someone is shooting people at a school in the very first sentence of your call. As the call progresses, be prepared to provide information about the number of people on campus at the time, the current location of the attacker, and any gate or door codes necessary to enter the property or building. If at all possible and safe, it is ideal to have someone available outside to meet arriving officers with a master key to the facility; this will help the officers expedite their entry to various parts of the school and save them from having to take the time to manually breach any locked doors they encounter. Remember that each second counts and the quicker law enforcement officers can stop an attack, the more lives will be saved.

Communication also needs to take place within your building to alert all occupants about an armed attacker in the area. As previously discussed, now is the time to implement your internal communication plan that alerts all students, staff, and faculty about the situation. PA systems and handheld radios are ideal, but if they are not accessible or working, simply yelling clear and concise information to others will suffice. People need to know what is going on and where in order to help them determine what actions to take next.

During training sessions I conduct for area schools, I am often asked about pulling fire alarms as a way to alert others that an attack is taking place in the building. In most cases, I believe that activating fire alarms in a school attack situation is a bad idea and will do more harm than good. While it does alert building occupants that an emergency is taking place, it funnels the entire population of the school out from their locked classrooms and into what would likely be a kill zone. From here panic would almost certainly ensue and teachers would have a very difficult time accounting for their students.

When you do hear a fire alarm activated within your school, you should instruct your students to form a line near your door but not to exit immediately. As a teacher, you should view the area immediately outside of your classroom and beyond to confirm the source of the alarm is legitimate, if at all possible. In order to accomplish this, attempt to communicate with your peers or front office administrative staff through whatever means your administration has previously established. This can be via text message, cell phone, or portable radios. If staff members share specific concerns over the legitimacy of the alarm, proceed cautiously during your evacuation procedures.

ESCAPE

While you are on the phone with 9-1-1 and also communicating to others around you, it is important to implement the first option of your response plan: escape the area of the shooting. If it is safe to do so, exit the building with your students in the most expeditious fashion and get as far away from the location and threat as possible. Your rendezvous location could be a major street, an adjacent building, a nearby parking lot, or even a wooded area nearby. Your facility parking lot is not a good rally point due to the possibility of destructive devices placed in the parking lot, as well as the parking lot's close proximity to the site of the attack.

While on your way out, communicate the

situation to any people you come across in your pathway. Also encourage them to follow you if they don't react in a manner that reflects the reality of the situation. You may come across students, staff, and teachers who are frozen by fear and panic, which will make it necessary for you to snap them out of their stupor. You may have to yell, push, or physically coerce them to follow you to safety.

In an escape situation like this, you should use the most reasonable escape route given the circumstances and building layout you are faced with. You must also consider the age and physical capabilities of your students when making your decision to escape. The younger your students, the more time you will need to escape and provide directions. If you teach special needs students who are physically or mentally disabled, you will also need more time to conduct your escape. If you don't feel completely confident with your entire classroom's ability to successfully escape, you should begin planning to deny the attacker access to you and your students, which we will discuss in the next section.

If you are able to escape from the area you are in through any standard entrance or exit door without encountering the perpetrator, this should be your first option. You are responsible for directing your class out of the building in an orderly fashion and making sure they follow your directions exactly as you say them. The most important thing here is to stay calm despite what is going on around you. Your students and peers will cue off of your mental state and reactions; if you stay calm, the large majority of them will stay calm. If you begin to panic and scream, they will do the same. Be sure to reassure your students that they will be safe as long as they stay with you and listen to your instructions.

While some classrooms are near entrances and exits, the large majority will not be. Even if you are able to make it to a major entrance or exit, school attackers have been known to block or barricade exits to increase the possibility of creating additional carnage. If you find yourself in a classroom far from any logical exit, you have two options depending on the physical properties of your classroom. The very first thing you should do, regardless of the location of your classroom, is to shut and lock (or otherwise secure) your door, and turn off all lights within the area you are located. If your door has windows on it or near it, you should cover them with some sort of previously installed lockdown window

Blinds like these are an excellent method of keeping the contents of your classroom concealed. Simple drop covers serve the same purpose for budget-minded teachers and districts.

covering. These covers can be as complex as mini-blinds or as simple as non-transparent fabric secured to the door or window with Velcro or magnets.

If your classroom does not have a door that you can lock from the inside, this needs to be immediately addressed with your administration and maintenance staff. Doors that lock securely from the inside without a key should be mandatory on all classroom and office doors. Teachers should not be forced to step in the hallway or find their keys to lock the door in a moment of extreme stress. According to the final Sandy Hook report, all interior classroom doors in the Sandy Hook elementary school locked from the outside with a key and the interior door handles had no locking mechanism. A teacher at Sandy Hook named Victoria Soto was killed by the attacker within only a few feet of her keys, which were required to lock her classroom door. Had Ms. Soto been able to easily lock her door from the inside, her outcome and the outcome of her students may have been more positive. Having classroom doors that are equipped to easily lock from the inside is the bare minimum that is required to protect teachers and students in the event of an armed school attack; teachers should make it clear to their administrators and school boards that appropriate locks on classroom doors are mandatory.

Once you have secured your classroom and covered any interior window, you should instruct all of your students to stay extremely quiet so the attention of the attacker is not called to the classroom. If you have an exterior facing window and your classroom is located on the first or second floor of your school, you should immediately make plans to break the window and exit the building. While the possibility exists that more than one person could conduct an attack, only 8 percent of school shootings studied in the Safe School Initiative2 final report were conducted by two or more perpetrators. Statistically speaking, the odds are extremely small that an additional shooter or shooters will be outside waiting for children to escape. Based on the events to date, your chances for survival increase significantly if you and your children escape the building as quickly as possible if an attacker is inside the school. Even if secondary attackers are outside of the building, their success rate of hitting long-distance moving targets will be significantly lower than close-range targets confined within a classroom.

While many things in a classroom can be used to break a window, nothing is as efficient as a small and inexpensive tool designed specifically to break glass. Every classroom on the first and second floor with an exterior window should have a glass-breaking tool available within the room.

The LifeHammer is a small sized window-breaking device designed for automobile applications but is excellent in breaking all types of

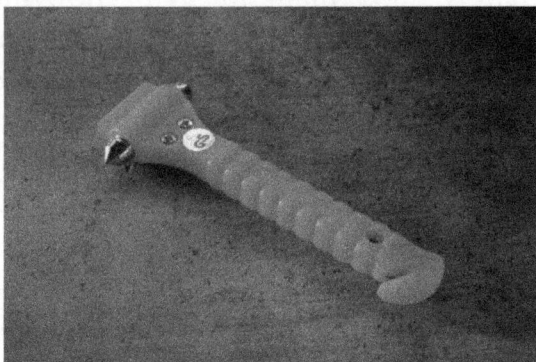

The LifeHammer is readily available, extremely cost-effective, and an exceptionally capable glass-breaking device.

glass, not just automotive glass. I have personally tested over a dozen different glass breakers and the LifeHammer performed the best by far. I have tested it on both plate and tempered glass of varying thicknesses, including glass that is significantly thicker that what is found in the large majority of commercial buildings, including schools. The LifeHammer clearly performed the best out of all glass breakers tested, and even broke double-paned glass with ease, which will save you precious time during a school attack. The hammer sells for approximately $15 and should be stored in an easily accessible place in every classroom. It is readily available for sale on many online websites, including Amazon.

Since it is designed for automotive applications, it is also embedded with a small razor blade for cutting seat belts. Considering razor blades and schools are often a bad combination, the blade can easily be removed by unscrewing three screws with a Philips screwdriver. Each hammer should be stored in the same or similar location in each classroom, so all teachers (full-time and substitutes) know where to find them. After providing a local preschool with a presentation on this topic, they purchased LifeHammers for each classroom and stored it in the same location in each classroom, mounted near the clock within reach of adults, but out of reach for little curious hands.

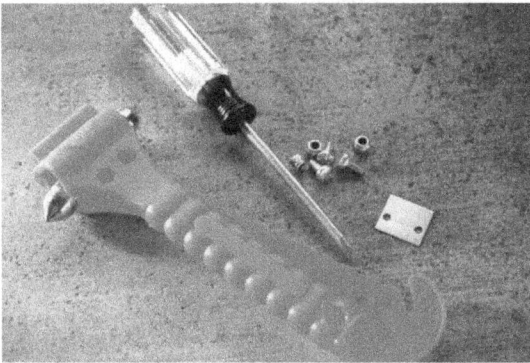

The LifeHammer can easily be disassembled in order to remove the seatbelt cutting blade from within.

Most schools have either single-pane or double-pane tempered glass installed on exterior windows. The weakest point of glass is on its edge, making it important to strike the glass with a glass breaker near the edge for an easy break. Tempered glass is designed to break into thousands of tiny pieces that significantly reduce the risk of any sort of significant cut to your hand or body. Once you break the glass, you should help all of your students out of the window and direct them where to run. Some students may experience small cuts or scrapes while exiting the window, but injuries like this pale in comparison to the alternative.

Making an escape from a first-story window is an extremely easy decision when facing a school attacker armed with guns, but a second-floor classroom adds a level of possible injury to the equation. While second-floor window heights can vary from school to school based on architecture, many would fall within the 15–30 foot range. Making the decision to exit a school from a second-story window may not necessarily be as easy some would think. Your student's age and physical development will play an important role in the decision-making process. Kindergarteners would not fare as well in a second-floor fall as a senior in high school, but both would more than likely live and suffer only relatively minor injuries.

In a school attack situation in which the perpetrator is attempting entrance to your specific classroom or even shooting through a door or window at you and your students, the alternative to a second-story fall is serious injury and almost certain death. Personally, I'd much rather pay for my children's medical bills for a broken leg or ankle, than have to bury them. Small lead projectiles traveling at 2,000 feet per second are guaranteed to cause much more severe injuries than a second-story fall. Rest assured I have given permission to my children's teachers to keep them safe through any means possible, even if it means helping them with a controlled fall out of a window on the second story of their school.

DENY

If you are caught in a situation where escape through an entrance or exit is not possible and you are not in an area with windows that you can escape from, your next best option is to deny the attacker access to yourself and your students. This denial often comes in two forms:

barricading or hardening the immediate area you and your students are in, and concealing yourselves from view of the attacker. As previously discussed, this should be behind a door that is locked from the inside with any interior windows covered and lights turned off. Once the door is secured, it can be beneficial to barricade the door with desks, chairs, bookshelves, and any other heavy objects that can impede and slow entry into your area. Barricading is most effective on doors that open to the inside, although it can help to slow entry even if the door opens by swinging out. If moving furniture becomes too noisy it could potentially draw the attacker's attention to your classroom so it is important to move quickly and not spend too much time doing this, especially if you have a door that can be locked from the inside. If your door locks from the inside, it is more beneficial to not draw attention to your classroom by staying quiet than to noisily move heavy furniture in front of a door that may already be difficult to breach.

If your classroom does not have a window that you can exit out of, you may be near an internal storm or emergency shelter that is somehow fortified. If denying access becomes your only option because you can't make it to an exit of some sort, consider proceeding to an internal shelter area if available and safe. These rooms can include high-strength lockable doors or even strong roll-down fortified storm doors.

Once you lock and fortify your immediate area, students should begin hiding behind large objects, including overturned desks and in-storage cabinets or closets if available. Staying quiet and calm continues to be important at this point, so as a teacher it is important to stay level headed so your students cue off of your emotions. Silence in your classroom includes silencing cell phones and calming students who are having trouble maintaining their composure. Reassuring students in a calm voice that they will be safe as long as they listen to you will go a long way. While you and your students are hiding, everyone (depending on your student's ages) should be preparing for the possibility of fighting an attacker, should they successfully breach your location and attempt to harm you. While hiding, the teacher should discuss the possibility of fighting off the attacker should he make entrance to the room, if the students are of a sufficient age to follow directions and be effective at the tasks they are given. Once a perpetrator makes it in a classroom, any resistance is better than no resistance at all.

During the training sessions I conduct, I've often been asked about the viability of playing dead during an attack. While this is certainly on the spectrum of possibilities for reaction, it is not something that I would typically advise. If an attacker makes it into your area and you play dead, you have given complete control of the rest of your life to the attacker. If you choose to fight the attacker, you at least have a chance at controlling your own destiny through an aggressive means of defending yourself and your students. Again, playing dead allows the attacker to decide if you live or die, which is obviously the worst-case scenario.

There are certain limited circumstances in which playing dead has worked in the past, although victims often survive based on advances in emergency medicine, versus attackers choosing not to shoot the victims any more than they already have. A prime example of this is Kristina Anderson who was in one of the classrooms targeted by the Virginia Tech mass murderer in 2007. In this situation, the attacker entered her classroom and began shooting numerous students, including Ms. Anderson herself who was shot once. Once the shooter left her classroom he returned shortly thereafter, at which point

Ms. Anderson decided she would attempt to play dead hoping the attacker would not shoot her again. During his second attack on Ms. Anderson's classroom, she was shot two more times. Luckily Ms. Anderson survived all three gunshots, though she still lives today with physical and emotional scars. Advances in medical technology likely saved Ms. Anderson's life because the Virginia Tech mass murderer was so set on killing as many people as possible that he felt it necessary to kill everyone he came in contact with. Ms. Anderson was very fortunate to survive this attack, although others who attempt to play dead may not fare so well.

FIGHT

Fighting off a mass murderer is typically your last resort and should be carried out in the most violent fashion you are capable of. This is horrible and outrageous to think about, but absolutely necessary if you want the best chance of saving your life and the lives of your students. As troubling as it is to think about, overwhelming violence against the perpetrator is the only thing that will stop their reprehensible actions. You have to remember at this point that you are face to face with someone who thinks that murdering innocent children and adults is the answer to their problems. They have no respect for the lives of others and are clearly not capable of feeling any sort of empathy or compassion for others.

Most school murderers are sociopaths with no remorse and have a long history of manipulating, violating, and exploiting others. It should make you extremely angry that a low-life attacker has put you in the position in which you have to react with overwhelming violence and aggression to stop their senseless actions. Like a mama bear protecting her cubs, you should stop at nothing to protect yourself and your students. Channel the anger you feel toward them and fight hard to stop their cowardly actions. While you may be feeling the highest level of fear in your life, turning your fear into rage will help you and your students survive through the attack.

While you are hiding in your classroom, you should immediately begin looking for weapons that you can use to increase your advantage over an attacker armed with a gun or knife. Anything that can harm, weaken, or distract the attacker will work in a situation like this. Ideally you would already have a general idea of what is available to use as a weapon in your classroom, which you would accomplish during your preparation phase of training. Thinking of things like this in advance will shorten your decision-making process during a true emergency.

This book is not focused on teaching you specific defensive tactics, but you should at least be aware of what general actions you can take to fight back and protect yourself and your students. Heavy blunt objects like fire extinguishers and paperweights can be effective if thrown at an attacker, or can be used to hit an attacker at close range. Smaller sharp objects like scissors can also prove beneficial if you are within arm's reach of the individual. In many situations, it is also beneficial for all of the occupants in the room to throw books and other objects in unison, which can distract the attacker enough that a teacher or older student can attempt to tackle or further disable the aggressor.

Targeting an attacker's face can be especially beneficial because general human nature tells us that things hitting us in the face are bad and should be avoided. Books and other objects thrown at an attacker's face will almost certainly result in them trying to block them with their hands, which means they don't have their hands on their gun or knife to continue attacking. While only temporary, this can give a teacher or older students the advantage to further attack the perpetrator, possibly take their gun from them, and stop their actions permanently.

There have been circumstances where teachers have successfully fought back against attackers, thus stopping further deaths and injuries. An excellent example of this is the attack that happened at Chardon High School in Chardon, Ohio, on February 27, 2012. During this attack, a seventeen-year-old attacker entered the school's cafeteria with a handgun and fired ten times, wounding two students and killing three others. Upon hearing the shots, teacher Frank Hall charged the attacker and chased him out of the school, despite the fact that the attacker pointed his gun at Hall on multiple occasions. Hall's selfless actions and indomitable spirit likely saved the lives of countless students. Additionally, one of Hall's fellow teachers, Joseph Ricci, also acted in a courageous manner during the attack. When Ricci heard gunshots in the school, he immediately locked down his students in their classroom. Shortly after, he heard moaning coming from outside his classroom door. He opened the door to find a wounded student, at which point he dragged the student inside his classroom and began to administer first aid, saving the student's life.

In another recent school shooting, teacher Megan Silberberger confronted a fourteen-year-old attacker who began shooting at students in the cafeteria of Marysville-Pilchuck High School in Marysville, Washington, on October 24, 2014. Media reports indicate that as soon as Silberberger heard the shots in her school, she rushed to the area; what happens next is where eyewitness accounts differ. Some say Silberberger grabbed the arm of the attacker while he was trying to target more students, causing the attacker to try to pull his arm away from her, resulting in the attacker fatally shooting himself in the neck. Other accounts mention Silberberger was not in any sort of physical altercation with the attacker, but approached him while yelling, "Stop! Stop! Stop," at which point the attacker turned the gun on himself.

These three recent examples of teachers who took action and saved the lives of countless students and peers shows that a little bit of mental preparation and quick thinking go a long way in situations like these.

As obvious as it sounds, you must understand that now is not the time to fight fair. Your own life and the lives of your students are in your hands when you come face-to-face with someone intent on killing as many people as possible. If you make the choice to fight, you must do so with the greatest amount of violence imaginable if you expect to prevail over someone who has the distinct advantage of a firearm or knife over you. Now is the time to kick, punch, scratch, eye gouge, and bite. Imagine how effective biting an attacker's face or hands would be. As gross or violent as it may sound, when lives are on the line and you are at a disadvantage, you must make every available advantage work for you.

Fighting back is a personal choice that every person must make based on their life experience, physical conditioning, and their self-perceived level of aggressiveness. When facing an armed assailant, the chances are high that you may be injured or even killed; however once an attacker moves into your immediate area, your chances of being injured or killed are likely equally as high, if not higher. If you are concerned that you don't know how to fight if given the chance, you should consider taking some self-defense classes from a local police department or martial arts training facility. You shouldn't be intimidated; many places often hold self-defense courses designed specifically for people who have little to no experience on the topic. They may also provide a discounted rate for teachers and anyone who can get a small group of friends to attend the class together. Get a group of colleagues and friends together for a night out to attend a class and go to dinner. Have fun with it and make it a bonding experience together.

Fighting back is centered around protecting yourself and your students if you come face-to-face with an armed attacker. This does not include searching for or hunting down the armed attacker. Hunting down the attacker is not advisable because you open yourself up to extreme risk and you could potentially complicate the situation when responding law enforcement officers arrive on-scene.

As we have discussed throughout this chapter, you have three primary reactions to choose from when faced with an armed attacker: escape, deny, or fight. Escaping the area of the attack should always be the first priority if possible, because your odds of survival increase as you move further away from the area of the attack.

Denying the attacker access to you and your

students involves locking and barricading the door to your immediate area, turning off lights, and concealing your location within the room by staying quiet and covering windows, if possible.

Fighting off attackers is a personal choice that must be made based on your confidence in your physical and mental capabilities. Fighting gives you the ability to potentially change the course of the shooter's actions in a positive way, instead of letting the shooter decide if he wants to continue to create more victims. You have the power to assess your specific situation and make an educated decision about which course of action to take, given the circumstances you find yourself in. Quick, educated decision-making, coupled with an indomitable spirit, will give you and your students a significant advantage and increase your odds of survival exponentially.

CHAPTER SEVEN:
POWER OF MIND
OVER BODY

If you make the decision to fight, you must also understand that the likelihood of some sort of injury is high. Injuries can range from minor to life-threatening, but keeping a positive mental outlook and fighting through your injuries is completely possible. Human bodies are capable of withstanding huge amounts of abuse; just watch any mixed martial arts match. The DNA that makes these fighters human is the exact same DNA that is contained within your body. The difference is that these fighters have trained themselves to persevere through extreme pain and injury. It is absolutely possible to fight through and survive significant injuries, even multiple gunshots, if you maintain a strong mind and positive mental outlook.

If you don't believe me, let's take a look at a prime example of the power of mind over body. Master Sergeant (MSG) Roy Benavidez was awarded the United States' highest military honor, the Congressional Medal of Honor, on February 24, 1981, for his exceptional actions in Loc Ninh, Vietnam, on May 2, 1968. The following are excerpts from his complete award citation, as reported in Benavidez' autobiography[8]:

On May 2, 1968, Master Sergeant (Staff Sergeant) Roy P. Benavidez distinguished himself by a series of daring and extremely valorous actions while assigned to Detachment B56, 5th Special Forces Group (Airborne), 1st Special Forces, Republic of Vietnam. On the morning of May 2, 1968, a 12 man Special Forces Reconnaissance Team was inserted by helicopters in a dense jungle area west of Loc Ninh, Vietnam to gather intelligence information about confirmed large-scale enemy activity. This area was controlled and routinely patrolled by the North Vietnamese Army. After a short period of time on the ground, the team met heavy enemy resistance, and requested emergency extraction.

Sergeant Benavidez voluntarily boarded a returning aircraft to assist in another extraction attempt. Realizing that all the team members were either dead or wounded and unable to move to the pickup zone, he directed the aircraft to a nearby clearing where he jumped from the hovering helicopter, and ran approximately 75 meters under withering small arms fire to the crippled team. Prior to reaching the team's position he was wounded in his right leg, face, and head. Despite these painful injuries, he took charge, repositioned the team members and directed their fire to facilitate the landing of an extraction aircraft, and the loading of wounded and dead team members.

Despite his severe wounds and under intense enemy fire, he carried and dragged half of the wounded team members to the waiting aircraft. He then provided protective fire by running alongside the aircraft as it moved to pickup classified documents on the dead team leader. When he reached the team leader's body, Sergeant Benavidez was severely wounded by small arms fire in the abdomen and grenade fragments in his back.

At nearly the same moment, the aircraft pilot was mortally wounded and his helicopter crashed. Although in extremely critical condition due to his wounds, Sergeant Benavidez secured the classified documents and made his way back to the wreckage, where he aided the wounded out of the overturned aircraft, and gathered the stunned survivors into a defensive perimeter.

Under increasing automatic weapons and grenade fire, he moved around the perimeter distributing water and ammunition to his weary men, reinstilling in them a will to live and fight. Facing a buildup of enemy opposition with a beleaguered team, Sergeant Benavidez mustered his strength, began calling in tactical air strikes and directed the fire from supporting gunships to suppress the enemy fire and so permit another extraction attempt. He was wounded again in his thigh by small arms fire while administering first aid to a wounded team member just before another extraction helicopter was able to land. His indomitable spirit kept him going as he began to ferry his comrades to the craft.

On his second trip with the wounded, he was clubbed from behind by an enemy soldier. In the ensuing hand-to-hand combat, he sustained additional wounds to his head and arms before killing his adversary. He then continued under devastating fire to carry the wounded to the helicopter. Upon reaching his aircraft, he spotted and killed two enemy soldiers who were rushing the craft from an angle that prevented the air-craft door gunner from firing upon them.

With little strength remaining, he made one last trip to the perimeter to ensure that all classi-fied material had been collected or destroyed, and to bring in the remaining wounded. Only then, in extremely serious condition from numerous wounds and loss of blood, did he allow himself to be pulled into the extraction aircraft. Sergeant Benavidez' gallant choice to join voluntarily his comrades who were in critical straits, to expose himself constantly to withering fire, and his refusal to be stopped despite numerous severe wounds, saved the lives of at least eight men.

If that citation doesn't paint the picture of the power of mind over body, a positive mental outlook, and a will to survive, nothing does. During this one battle, Benavidez received a total of thirty-seven wounds of varying degrees from bullets, shrapnel, and bayonets. This was in addition to having a broken jaw and being eviscerated by a bullet wound, forcing him to hold his own intestines in his abdomen during the latter portions of the battle. Benavidez later wrote that he had shrapnel in his head, scalp, shoulder, buttocks, feet, and legs, bullets had entered his back, one exiting beneath his heart, and another bullet had entered his lower right back. Enemy soldier's bayonets had also slashed both of his arms. After the evacuation helicopter landed back at base, Benavidez was placed into a body bag by fellow soldiers who thought he had deceased, based on his physical appearance. While zipping up the body bag, a doctor placed his hand on Benavidez' chest to feel for a heartbeat, which is when Benavidez spit in his face to communicate that he was still alive. Indomitable spirit indeed!

It should be noted, however, that these were not MSG Benavidez' first combat-related injuries while in Vietnam. According to his autobiography, several years earlier Benavidez had stepped on a landmine that deformed his spine, leaving him paralyzed, and shattered numerous pieces of bone and cartilage throughout his body. When he first awoke in the hospital, his doctors informed him he was paralyzed and would never walk again. While recovering from his severe wounds in the hospital, he was not

MSG Roy P. Benavidez's book,
in which he relays his life experiences.

afforded any type of physical therapy designed
to help him walk again because the medical staff
thought it was not medically possible for him to
do so. Benavidez was determined to walk again
and serve his country, so at night he began his
own regimen of painful self-employed physical
therapy, trying to change his fate and walk again.
Each night Benavidez would fall out of bed, hold
himself up with his arms placed on top of two
nightstands, and attempt to stand and walk in
excruciating pain. After several months of this
nightly ritual, Benavides was able to walk and
move enough that he could convince the Army
to qualify him for at least limited duty, even
though he was in constant pain.

Roy Benavidez was not superhuman but did display actions that made it appear as though he was. What made Benavidez an absolute hero was the mental strength and determination he held. The power of the human mind is amazing and Benavidez' story is a prime example of the trauma a human body can endure, so long as the mind is capable of pushing it to do so.

CHAPTER EIGHT:
LAW ENFORCEMENT RESPONSE

Prior to the Columbine school shooting in 1999, law enforcement response to a mass murder or active shooter situation was for responding patrol officers to essentially secure the perimeter of a structure and call the SWAT team who would then enter the building and stop the shooter through the use of whatever force necessary. This was based on the training and equipment (or lack thereof) of the era in which it happened. In the Columbine situation, this allowed the shooters to wander their campus and murder teachers and children at will for approximately

45 minutes. As anyone can see, a faster response from properly equipped law enforcement patrol officers could have saved a greater number of lives.

Today's active shooter training sessions for law enforcement teach a significantly more aggressive form of response with the number-one priority of stopping the perpetrator(s) before any other actions are taken. Officers are taught to use overwhelming force and violence to stop the aggressor from harming anyone else that may be in their path. Responding offers are now better equipped with breaching equipment, longer range firearms of various calibers, upgraded body armor, and superior training.

It is important to gain a general understanding of how responding law enforcement officers will react so you can prepare yourself and your students for what you will experience. The very first officers responding to the scene will immediately enter your school through whatever means possible. This can happen through an open door, or they may choose an alternate entry point like a window or other opening. Although not ideal, many departments allow their officers to make entry by themselves if backup is not immediately available or close. The more

The more likely scenario is that two or three officers will arrive within a few seconds of each other, quickly (within a few seconds) determine the best point of entry, and enter the school. Once inside, they will move directly to the sound of the gunfire or commotion so they can engage and stop the aggressor. Along their way to the aggressor, they will bypass all wounded individuals because their most important task is to stop the killer from harming others.

Upon making entry into the school, officers are typically working off of limited information, some of which may be conflicting. Police dispatchers will constantly update responding officers with real-time information and considering the people reporting the information are human, sometimes the information isn't 100 percent accurate. It is for this reason that officers will treat anyone they come into contact with as a possible suspect until they make an assessment otherwise. With this understanding, you may have firearms pointed at you by responding officers and they may yell commands at you, your peers, and your students. It is extremely important to do exactly as you are told so the officers can assess the area and continue with their task at hand. Depending on the situation, you may also be handcuffed or otherwise immobilized by officers during the course of their response. You should not be upset or offended by the directive commands or immobilization; officers are simply trying to create order out of chaos and your cooperation will aid the process.

Officers may also push you down or in a different direction if they feel you are in some sort of imminent danger. If you are fleeing the building and an officer instructs you to take an alternate route, do so unless you know the attacker is in that direction. The only time you should engage the officers in a conversation or communicate with them is to inform them of where the attacker is, if you know this information. If this is the case, quickly tell them where you last saw the perpetrator, what he was wearing, and what he was doing. At this point, any other information is likely irrelevant, including how many people are injured or dead, because that information will not help officers stop the threat any more quickly. Asking officers questions or informing them that you need help is senseless; they know you need help which is why they were called there in the first place. Once you have relayed this vital bit of information, continue on your escape path so the officers can continue with their task at hand.

While escaping or denying access, don't yell or scream to cope with the situation. This will further complicate the circumstances by making communication more difficult and possibly prompting others to act in a similar fashion. It is also important to keep your hands visible when coming into contact with responding officers. Law enforcement officers are trained to watch people's hands because hands are typically the only thing that can cause them harm. Hands can hold guns, knives, bombs, and other things that can make an officer's day go south. By keeping your hands up and visible, officers can see you are likely not an immediate threat to them, which allows them to scan the area for people or things that are an actual threat.

Once officers do encounter the attacker and terminate his actions, either through peaceful negotiation or through deadly force, you should be prepared to shelter in place while the entire building is "cleared" by law enforcement. "Clearing" is the meticulous process of canvassing the entirety of the building, inside and out, looking for anyone else who may be hiding with the intent to further harm others. Clearing typically involves teams of officers moving from room to room, searching the building for other perpetrators or items the perpetrators left that may cause further harm, like bombs or other incendiary devices. Depending on the size of the school and number of officers available to conduct the search, this process usually takes several hours. Once the entire building is made safe, medical personnel are then allowed in the building to triage and treat victims. If officers find victims gravely wounded during their search, they'll likely conduct basic first aid (i.e., stop the bleeding) and possibly even evacuate the victim to a predetermined safe area where medical personnel are waiting to treat casualties.

Since the clearing process can take hours, as a teacher you must be prepared to render basic first aid to yourself and your students if necessary. While medical instruction is beyond the scope of this book, pressure over wounds is universally known to slow or stop bleeding, and tourniquets are safe to use to slow or stop bleeding from extremities like arms or legs, and can easily be fashioned out of belts, rope, power cords, or anything else flexible. If it isn't already a requirement for your employment as a teacher, many places like the Red Cross or your local hospital offer free or low-cost first aid classes. If you get enough peers interested, instructors may even travel to your school to conduct free on-site training for larger groups.

Many schools employ one or more nurses on a full-time basis. In conjunctions with the continuing education requirements, these nurses are mandated to keep their licenses in good standing, and they should seek out classes focused on trauma assessment and treatment. These classes often focus on the use of life-saving devices such as tourniquets and trauma dressings to increase the likelihood of survival. Once trained, each school nurse's office should be properly equipped with a sufficient amount of tourniquets and trauma bandages for use in the event of a mass shooting on campus. These life-saving simple devices are relatively inexpensive and when purchased at a district or multi-school level for all schools in an area, can be obtained even cheaper at a bulk discount rate.

AFTERWORD:
YOU HAVE THE POWER

Relatively speaking, armed school attacks are a low-probability, high-consequence event that must be planned for. Armed attacks on schools have increased significantly over the last ten years and you must be prepared to react appropriately if ever faced with a violent attack. It has been decades since anyone has died in a school fire, yet we continue to build our schools with fire-resistant materials and conduct periodic fire drills with students and faculty. These measures all contribute to the lack of deaths related to fire, and they should continue to be implemented.

As a teacher, you are responsible for your safety and the safety of those around you. Reading this book is an excellent first step in preparing yourself to react to an armed attacker, but I encourage you to pursue additional local training in some of the topics we covered.

During an armed attack in your school, you are not helpless; quite to the contrary, you actually have the power to change the outcome of the situation. Law enforcement is often only minutes away, but every second counts so you must rehearse and implement what you have learned. Remember that your students and peers will cue off of your emotions, so it is important to stay calm. Intentionally slowing your breathing into deep methodical rhythms will bring your heart rate down, which will allow you to think, react, and communicate more clearly. If you find yourself injured during an attack, remember what Master Sergeant Benavides taught us about the power of mind over body. You can persevere through even the most debilitating of injuries if you maintain a positive mental attitude and indomitable spirit.

Escape is always the most ideal option but if the opportunity does not exist, you must deny the attacker access to you and your students. If the attacker manages to gain access to you and your students, you must make the personal decision to fight off the attacker by turning your fear into rage. Again, you have the ability to act and change the outcome.

Preparation, quick thinking, and courage will help give you an advantage and increase your chances of survival. No matter what situation you are faced with, you have the potential to change the course of action and bring calm during the storm. Share this book with others, mentally prepare for potential situations within your school and everyday life, and nurture the indomitable spirit that lives within you.

RESOURCES

1. United States Active Shooter Events from 2000 to 2010: Training and Equipment Implications. (March 2013). J. Pete Blair, Ph.D., Director of Research, Advanced Law Enforcement Rapid Response Training (ALERRT), Texas State University and M. Hunter Martaindale, Ph.D. Student, School of Criminal Justice, Texas State University.

2. The Final Report and Findings of the Safe School Initiative: Implications for the Prevention of School Attacks in the United States. (May 2002). United States Secret Service and United

States Department of Education. Bryan Vossekuil, Robert A. Fein, Ph.D., Marisa Reddy, Ph.D., Randy Borum, Psy.D., William Modzeleski.

3. The School Shooter: A Threat Assessment Perspective Critical Incident Response Group (CIRG), National Center for the Analysis of Violent Crime (NCAVC), FBI Academy, Quantico, VA 22135, Mary Ellen O'Toole, PhD, Supervisory Special Agent, FBI, undated.

4. Virginia Tech Review Panel. (2007). Mass shootings at Virginia Tech report of the review panel.

5. Vecchi, G.M. (2009). Conflict and crisis communication: Workplace and school violence, Stockholm syndrome, and abnormal psychology. Annals of the American Psychotherapy Association, 30-39.

6. Epstein, S. (1994). The Integration of the Cognitive and Psychodynamic Unconscious. American Psychologist, 49: 709-723.

7. Artwohl, A. (2002). FBI Law Enforcement Bulletin: Perceptual and Memory Distortion During Officer-Involved Shootings.

8. Benavidez, R., Craig, J. (1995). Medal of Honor: A Vietnam Warrior's Story.

ABOUT THE AUTHOR

Steven Remy is a law enforcement officer and freelance writer who lives in the Dallas-Ft. Worth metroplex of Texas. After receiving his Bachelor of Science degree in Sociology from Texas A&M University, he commissioned in the U.S. Air Force and became a criminal investigator for the U.S. Air Force Office of Special Investigations (AFOSI). After five years of service and multiple overseas combat deployments, Steven separated from the U.S. Air Force as a Captain and began working in private industry as a corporate security professional. Realizing his passion rested in working as a public servant, he returned to work as a federal law enforcement officer in the late 2000s where he currently works today.

Steven is a credentialed Certified Protection Professional (CPP) through ASIS International and holds a Master of Arts degree in Business and Organizational Security Management. In addition, he is also certified by the Federal Law Enforcement Training Center as a Basic Tactical Medical Instructor and an Active Shooter Threat Instructor.

"Those that cannot remember the past are condemned to repeat it."
—George Santayana

ABOUT LT. COL. DAVE GROSSMAN

Lt. Col. Dave Grossman is a former West Point psychology professor, Professor of Military Science, and an Army Ranger who is the author of *On Killing* (which was nominated by the publisher for a Pulitzer Prize), *On Combat* (with Loren Christensen), and *Stop Teaching Our Kids to Kill* (with Gloria DeGaetano). Col. Grossman's books have been translated into eight languages, and his books are required or recommended readings in colleges, military academies, and police academies around the world, to include the U.S. Marine Corps Commandant's reading list and the FBI Academy reading list. His research was cited by the President of the United States in a national address after the Littleton, Colorado school shootings, and he ha testified before the U.S. Senate, U.S. Congress, and numerous state legislatures. He has served as an expert witness and consultant in state and Federal courts, to include serving on the prosecution team in *UNITED STATES vs. TIMOTHY MCVEIGH.*

He helped train mental health professionals after the Jonesboro school massacre, and he was also involved in counseling or court cases in the aftermath of the Paducah, Springfield, and Littleton school massacres. He has been called upon to write the entry on "Aggression and Violence" in the *Oxford Companion to American Military History*, three entries in the *Academic Press Encyclopedia of Violence, Peace and Conflict,* and has presented papers before the national conventions of the American Medical Association, the American Psychiatric Association, the American Psychological Association, and the American Academy of Pediatrics.

Today he is the director of the Killology Research Group (www.killology.com), and in the wake of the 9/11 terrorist attacks he has been on the road almost 300 days year, training elite military and law enforcement organizations worldwide about the reality of combat, and he has written extensively on the terrorist threat with articles published in the Harvard Journal of Law and Public Policy and many leading law enforcement journals.

PRAISE FOR
INDOMITABLE SPIRIT

"I had the pleasure to work with Steve when implementing a new security plan for our preschool program. His knowledge and expertise was a valuable resource in creating policies and procedures to prepare for a threat against our school. His teacher training was full of information and helped the teachers understand their role in the event of an emergency. Although this is not a fun topic, it is a much-needed training for educators and schools."

Amy Stewardson, Director
Sunshine Kids Preschool

"Steven Remy's long-term experience in the field of law enforcement and security issues makes him a highly valued resource in today's world. In a time when public shootings and child abductions are more common than we would like to admit, it is essential that families, churches, schools, and other public facilities be prepared to respond. Steven Remy offers reasonable, affordable, and practical action items that a community can easily incorporate into its training and culture. We must ask, 'What does one do in the face of a crisis or threat?' Steven Remy has the answers."

Audrey Hair, MTS, Director of Worship
St. Gabriel the Archangel Catholic Community

www.ingramcontent.com/pod-product-compliance
Lightning Source LLC
Chambersburg PA
CBHW032354280326
41935CB00008B/574